A Guide to Creating Your Resume

or, "Resume I Help You?"

By Amy Rath

ISBN: 9798860581432

CONTENTS

Introduction

W hy write a book about resumes?

Short answer: because everyone deserves to have a well-crafted resume, no matter their background or experience. I've read and written hundreds of resumes and can help you create one that tells the world how great you are.

Longer answer: Once upon a time, I sorted through resumes and cover letters in my job at an Executive Search firm. In case you're not familiar with this type of organization, Executive Search firms fill open jobs for organizations. Typically, these are well-paying, high-level jobs with words like "Senior Executive" or "Vice President" in the title, requiring specific skills and experience. In today's world, a software program takes the first pass at scanning a resume, identifying key words and categorizing an individual based on what types of jobs they've worked. But several years ago, people like me did this work – so I read hundreds of long resumes from professionals who had achieved many things, and tried to figure out how to summarize what the people behind them knew how to do. The goal was to determine whether any of the jobs that our company was paid to fill were suitable for one of the people whose resume we'd received. I saw the time and attention offered to making folks who were already accomplished become even more so and realized that with some effort that any resume could become a better document.

After that job, I worked in Career Search, which is like the other side of the matching-jobs-and-people coin. In this field, you try to help individuals conduct a successful job search by providing services such as resume writing, and interview practice. In this role, rather than reading hundreds of resumes, I now wrote them. Working in Career Search gave me the opportunity to interact with folks from many roles at different companies and diverse life experiences. I learned how to format a person's background, interests, and expertise into a short, easy-to-read document which bragged to the world about their employable value. In this job, I realized that you didn't have to be a senior level executive to be a high-quality employee. I realized that resumes were meant to communicate the ways in which a person could help an organization achieve its goals, by describing what that individual most wanted to do.

From those two jobs, I learned that:

- Anyone can write a great resume.
- Most people have no idea how to do this.

Creating resumes is not a magical process. You don't need to be "a writer" and no matter what experience you do or do not have, you are worthy of a well-crafted resume. I truly believe that if I could learn how to write an effective resume, so can you. And this book will teach you how to write one.

So, why write a book about resumes?

Because it's not fair that this basic information isn't common knowledge. If most of us need jobs in order to live, and we need a resume in order to find a job, then we should know how to put together a resume.

So – let's learn how we do that.

Book Format

Book Format

This book is organized by the different sections of a resume. For each one we'll go into details regarding the purpose of that section, and related writing guidelines. There will be examples of what to do, and what NOT to do, as well as answers to common questions.

At the end you're given a resume example, which again breaks out the sections and highlights the most important suggestions for each.

While this book aims to be as detailed and thorough as possible, it's also meant to be efficient – meaning "not too long." This is because if you're working on creating a resume, then you probably want to spend your time getting it done instead of reading or scrolling for information. It might help you to focus on a section at a time; reading first, then trying to write your own; then proceeding to the next part - again reading first, then attempting your draft, and so on. That way you can create your resume as you move through the book; there's no need to wait until the end.

Sections of a Resume

The primary sections of a resume are:

    A. Header
    B. Summary (or Objective or Profile)
    C. Work Experience
    D. Education

Those sections tell the reader – meaning, the person with a job to fill – what they need to know to determine whether you are potentially a good fit for the job requirements or not. I like to think of your resume giving details to the question "May I help you?" by outlining specifically how you think you can help. Any other information, such as special hobbies, interests, and so on is likely irrelevant. Again, the purpose of a resume is to match you to the job you want, so my recommendation is to keep it as focused as possible. Ultimately, your resume is yours, so if you want to include additional sections then that is your choice – however we won't cover them in this book.

In each section I'll call out style choices for formatting and recommendations based on readability. My formatting choices are just that – choices. If any don't feel appropriate for your resume, then I encourage you to adjust to something you prefer. Recommendations based on ensuring your resume is easy to read and understand are accompanied by explanations clarifying why parts should be written a certain way. This book teaches the fundamentals of resume writing, so understanding the "why" behind the recommendations will help you learn how to apply these to your own resume.

Header

Header

The resume Header is your contact information. It is the first thing on the top of page one of your resume.

Example 1:

JAN DOERSON

Street • City, State Zip • 555-555-xxxx (c) • emailaddress@gmail.com

Example 2:

YOUR NAME

STREET, CITY, STATE, Zip
Phone: 123.456.7890 Email:

While there is no single "right" way to style your header, these are my recommendations. First, the header should be accurate, and easy-to-read. The reader will assume that you are comfortable being contacted using any of the information in the Header: your mailing address, phone number, or email. Therefore, when you are actively job searching and sharing your resume, you need to consistently check all these options – so you can communicate in a timely manner.

Your email address should be your own personal email account. If you are currently employed, then using your work email runs the risk of your job search being made public at work - which you might not want. If you are a student, using a school email address can increase the risk of messages from potential employers getting lost among other messages.   I recommend using an email address which is easily identifiable as you – so a combination of your name and other characters if necessary: Jan.A.Doerson1@email for example, indicates the email address likely belongs to someone named "Jan Doerson" and therefore is easy for the sender to associate with your resume.   I.Love.P1geons@email might be a fun and creative email account which you've had for years – but the odds of it being misspelled or mistaken for spam in a hiring manager's inbox are high.

Provide the phone number you are most likely to check – there typically isn't a need to provide both a home phone and a cell phone - even if you have a landline. During a job search, check your voice mail message to ensure that it is something you are comfortable with a potential employer hearing.   While in one of the examples above I show a (c) indicating a cell phone number, this is a style choice as opposed to a requirement.

Keep in mind that many resumes will be read by scanning software, so try to keep special characters in headings, such as creative spacers (*, •, -, and so on) or stylized underlining to a minimum. Use a standard "print" – as opposed to "script" font - and avoid one which is highly customized.   The main purpose of a Header is to identify you and provide your contact information; hiring managers or recruiters might read tens or even hundreds of resumes in a day, so keeping your information easy to read will be appreciated!

You can include your LinkedIn page, if you have one, since this is a very common site used by many professionals. If you include this information, make sure that your LinkedIn page is up to date enough that it matches your resume information. I would not recommend including any other social media pages, unless there is a site very specific to your profession which is commonly used, and which would help you land a job. Including this information is completely optional; in many cases a hiring manager might search for you on LinkedIn anyway, so including this in your Header can save them from having to figure out which profile is yours.

The Header is one area on a resume where you can buy more room on the page, if you need it. However, we don't want to be too obvious about it. Putting YOUR NAME in 20+ point font takes up a lot of room on the page – and shows the reader right off the top that you won't be using that room to talk about your skills and experience. However, using a slightly larger than normal font for your name, such as 14 point, and then spreading your name, address, and phone and email across three separate lines instead of two still consumes room on the page, but not in a way that looks as if there is nothing left for other information.

If your resume is longer than one page – for example, if you've been working for at least 5 to 7 years – then the second page will have a much more simplified Header. I recommend using only your name, written in a font the same size as the rest of your resume, and if desired a simple underline to separate it from the rest of the text (but that is optional and up to you). If someone prints out your resume, and it is on two pages, then you want it to be obvious that the second page still refers to "you." Alternately, if reading an electronic version, save them from having to scroll all the way back to the top of page 1 to remember your name. Again, imagine someone handling many resumes at a time as they review applicants for jobs; try to make it as easy as possible for the reader to understand whose information they are seeing.

If you are using page numbers in your resume, I recommend placing them in the lower corner in a footer, not in the Header. If your resume is a single page there is no need to use page numbers.

Here are a few examples of "Not to do's" – and why I recommend against them.

A. NO: Highly creative email addresses: I promise I'm not trying to stifle your personality. The primary reason for including an email address (and you absolutely should include one) is to make it easy for the hiring manager – who is most likely a stranger to you – to reliably get in contact with you. Using an email that is easily associated with you (such as your name) greatly reduces the chance of mistakes occurring – and you potentially missing an important message about a job!

B. NO: Multiple phone numbers and email addresses: Using your Header to provide a couple methods of making contact is ideal. Including 5 alternate phone numbers is completely unnecessary and confusing. If anything, this makes it seem as though it will be difficult to contact you, since who wants to try that many numbers just to hopefully get through?

C. NO: Photos as a part of your Header. Pictures will be difficult to scan and are not necessary.

D. NO: Extremely custom or difficult-to-read font. Again, this will be challenging to scan, likely difficult to read, and could result in someone not understanding your name or other information and being unable to contact you.

Summary

Summary (or Objective or Profile)

The next section of your resume is a short statement describing who you are, your top skills and interests, and what type of role you are looking for. Imagine someone reading only this section, and then stopping. What would you want them to remember about you? The reader will be wondering what you can offer their organization, so keep this in mind as you consider what to include in this section. I like to think of this as the opening of your "brag" document; so, let's talk about how to most effectively and quickly highlight the key points.

Example 1:

Profile

Organized, detail-oriented, ambitious individual returning to the workforce seeking to translate my skills to an office management role. Ideally looking to grow alongside a growing business.

Example 2:

SUMMARY AND OBJECTIVE

Warehouse staff with shift management experience and appreciation for a fast-paced environment. Goal of applying previous experience to a retail environment. Open to non-traditional hours.

Example 3 (includes <<blanks>> for you to fill in):

SUMMARY

High-performing, experienced <<<type of role>> committed to an opportunity which will utilize my skills <<name one or two>>, to positively impact individual, team, and organizational goals <<something you want to do that aligns with the roles you're applying for>>.

The opening section of your resume, which comes at the top of the page immediately following the header, goes by many terms. It doesn't matter whether you use Summary, or Objective, or Profile, but are the most common choices. The purpose, again, is to briefly highlight who you are (in the work world) and what type of job you're looking for.

This section should be brief, and it should make sense – which means that you don't have to use complete sentences. So, in the above examples, phrases like "looking for" rather than "I am looking for" are used. You'll find this throughout the resume – it's better to make statements descriptive and concise as opposed to grammatically perfect as if you were writing a book.

The way in which you describe your skills and interests should align with the type of role you want. If possible, you can borrow terms from a job posting; for example, if the company is looking for someone "with an attention to detail" then you might want to use the term "detail-oriented" in your description. Be sure to accurately represent yourself; don't claim that you love working with numbers and spreadsheets if math was your least favorite subject. Do not waste valuable word space noting anything you DON'T want to do; focus on the positive and pick two or three skills or accomplishments which you're proud of.

In the above examples I always center the section heading, no matter what term I use. This is my stylistic choice that I happen to think is the most visually appealing – but there is no rule saying this needs to be centered. I recommend leaving at least 1 line after the Header before the Summary, then 1 line after the word "Summary" (or Profile or Objective) before the remaining text. However, line spacing is another area where if you're concerned about having a shorter resume or less work experience then you might format this to be a line-and-a-half – but anything longer than that starts looking as if there is too much white space.

If you conduct a general internet search for resume examples online you might see some where this section appears on either the far right or far left of the page, as if in a sidebar. This can be difficult for scanning software to understand, and depending on how you create your document might not format correctly via email. To keep things straightforward, I recommend formatting like what I've provided in the examples above; it might be on the plain side, but it should almost always translate successfully via email, upload, download, print, and so on.

Because this section is so brief, every word counts. This is often the section where I spend the most amount of time; because you really want to ensure this gives the reader the best picture of what you can bring to a job. The Summary also helps set the tone for the rest of the resume. For example, if you are looking for a job in Sales, then make sure to mention this in the Summary and then highlight any relevant Sales experience in the next section, where we discuss your work. Or, if you're hoping to find a role managing others then this is something to call out as a part of your Objective, and then indicate times in which you've acted as a Manager or Team Leader in the following section.

It is okay in this section to use industry specific terms or acronyms if they are commonly recognized and understood. When in doubt, err on the side of clarity and spell things out so that you don't find yourself having to awkwardly explain in an interview something that might have been misunderstood.

Here are some suggestions of what "Not to do" in your Summary / Profile / Objective:

A. NO: Overly personal descriptions. Unless the information is incredibly specific for a particular job role, there is no reason to indicate whether you are married, single, young, older, your gender, cultural background, political affiliation, and so on.

B. NO: Inaccurate information. This pertains to your entire resume. What is highlighted in your Profile is what you will likely get hired to do; so, make sure that anything you represent is both factual and what you are looking for.

C. NO: Focusing on what you can't or haven't done. Your resume is your own professional showcase; there is no reason to put yourself down!

D. NO: "Education" does not immediately follow the Header – your Summary does. The only exception is if you currently are a student or have graduated within the last 12 months. Putting "Education" at the top of your resume tells the reader that this is the most important thing about you. If you are a student, then this might be true. If you are not, then Education goes at the end of your resume, after Work Experience.

Work Experience

Work Experience

This will be the longest portion of your resume. In this section you'll spell out where you worked, when, what you did, and what you're proud of. If there is one thing that I wish I could teach every single person who will ever need a resume, it is how to write bullets – meaning those short descriptions under the jobs listed in this section.

However, before we get to the bullets, we need to start with some basic information such as company name, role, and dates of employment. So, let's review some examples.

Example 1:

Work Experience

CORPORATION, City, State   2021 - Present
Corporation is a large retail chain, headquartered in Chicago.
Associate Consultant

Primary responsibilities include: reviewing data from multiple sources in order to create personalized dashboards for executives.

Example 2:

PROFESSIONAL EXPERIENCE

Data Entry Specialist (2021 – 2022)
COMPANY; Middletown, Ohio
Company is a small insurance office serving over 200 local customers.

Input documentation related to claims, and client communication for organized tracking. Also responsible for -

Let's start with the name of this section; I generally refer to it as "Work Experience," but "Professional Experience" is also fine. "Employment Experience" isn't commonly used, but it's another option. I recommend using which ever term feels more comfortable to you. If you have concerns, such as perhaps you are returning to the work world after a break, or this is your first "real" job, or for any reason you want something even more straightforward you can title this section "Experience."

As with the Summary I tend to center the title of this section just for a clean visual break, however this is a style choice and not a requirement. You can use bold font – or not, all capital letters – or not, but I would not recommend using a different size of font from the rest of your document. This is because a mixture of font sizes can look like a mistake as opposed to a deliberate choice; however, again, this is your document and no one else's.

Now, let's talk about sharing some important pieces of information; namely WHERE you worked (the name of the company), WHAT you did (your job title) and WHEN you worked there (dates of employment).

Your most recent and / or current employment goes first. It doesn't matter whether you start with the name of the company or your job title but be consistent for all the jobs in this section. So, if you start with the name of the company for your most recent job then start with the name of the company again for the job you had prior to this one, and so on. I like to have the name of the company and the job title on two separate lines to make each of them stand out. In the examples provided I use a mix of bold font and capital letters to again really make those key pieces of information – the company name and the job title – easy to pick out.

—

Put the location, generally city and state (written City, State) next to the company name. This helps the reader recognize whether you've moved at some point in time or consistently worked in the same area. Additionally, if the company isn't a well-recognized name, then this information is useful for research; I also recommend adding a brief description of the company. You can copy the company description directly off its website, but it only needs to be about one or two lines as opposed to a paragraph. Your resume should convey not only what you've specifically done in your job roles but also the type of organizations you've worked for, so both the location and a short description of the company are valuable.

The dates of employment come after either the name of the company, or the job title. I generally prefer to put these on the right-hand side of the page in order to make them easier to pick out. If you've worked at more than one job, then the reader can scan down the right-hand side of the page to quickly see all the years listed and, again, it is a nice, easy-to-read favor to format your resume in this way. But whether you choose to list these on the right or not, again be consistent with style throughout your resume.

Do not use the date format "2020 – Present" (or whatever the starting Year might be – Present) unless you are currently employed at that job at the time you are sending someone your resume. It could potentially be considered fraud if you indicate you are presently employed somewhere when you are not, so please ensure this is accurate.

I highly recommend listing years only, not months, in your dates. Look at these examples:

2020 – 2023

1997 – 2003

March, 2015 – July, 2018

In the first couple examples, you can quickly estimate how long someone was in a particular job. I'll tell you a secret: when I was regularly reading and writing hundreds of resumes, and even now as a hiring manager at my current company, I know that seeing dates like 2020 – 2023 might possibly mean "December of 2020 to February of 2023" and therefore the total amount of time at that job might be closer to two years than three – but it truly does not matter that much. As I've said before, imagine the reader is seeing lots of resumes; it is likely they are less interested in exactly when you started and ended a job as opposed to getting a general sense of your employment history. If they have questions for some reason about precisely when you started and ended, they can ask you.

Now, in the example above where both months and years are displayed, you probably tried to calculate exactly how long this was as you read it. Your brain devoted a little energy to figuring out whether this was over, under, or exactly three years and how many months were included in this timing. Typically, it's a more complex mental process to understand this timeframe than one showing only the years, which can mean that this part of your resume is difficult to read. This also can potentially cause unnecessary questions – for example, let's say you saw this on a resume:

Job 1 (March 2017 – June 2019)

—

Job 2 (July 2019 – December 2020)

Does this mean that this person was unemployed for most of the month of June or July? Did they end on June 30 and begin on July 1? There are significant American holidays in early July – did they start work in the middle of the month? The responses to these questions probably are not relevant to getting hired for a new role – however by writing the dates this way it could cause someone to wonder what you're trying to communicate. As opposed to writing it like this:

Job 1 (2017 – 2019)

Job 2 (2019 – 2020)

Indicates that sometime in 2019 this person changed from Job 1 to Job 2, which is likely all the reader needs to know regarding the timing of employment.

One thing we haven't discussed yet is how to handle dates when you've held more than one job at the same company. In this situation, reference the overall start and end dates for the entire time that you were employed by that company near the company name, and then the dates for each role by the appropriate job title. For the sake of cleaner formatting, I recommend always leading with the company name on the top line, then following with the individual job titles beneath. Here is an example.

Example 1:

As with everything else on your resume, the focus should be on communicating clearly and accurately the wonderful things you have done. This, I believe, is more important than diligently following any single set of formatting rules. The reader wants to get to know you and understand what you could contribute to their company, so our focus is on effectively sharing this information.

Let's move on to talking about job descriptions, responsibilities, and accomplishments.

Example 1:

EXPERIENCE

CURRENT COMPANY, City, State   2015 - Present
<<A brief description of the company – for example:>>
Leading provider of enterprise cloud applications for Finance and Human Resources.

Your Current Title
The first sentence should ideally contain something eye-catching, like numbers. For example:
Managed over $12.5MM of total account value for some of COMPANY's top customers in the Midwest.
Directly responsible for $360K new opportunity revenue.

- Now, write bullets. They do not need to be complete sentences. Bullets are easier to read than paragraphs.
- Try to have at least 2 to 3 bullets. Only include things you enjoy doing. If someone asks you about a bullet, be prepared to briefly describe in a positive way.

Example 2:

PROFESSIONAL EXPERIENCE

ORGANIZATION, City, State   2021 - 2024

Pet care and pet supply franchise.

Shift Manager

Responsible for scheduling 12 employees for AM shift, 6 days per week. Responsible for collecting timesheets, vacation tracking, and ensuring special events are staffed appropriately.

- Train new hires on stocking, cash register, and basic customer service knowledge.
- Act as escalation resource for complex customer inquiries.

Remember, when writing a resume, imagine asking the reader, "May I help you?" and then use the resume to explain the ways in which you can help. In the above example of a shift manager for a pet care store, the skills training new staff, managing staff schedules, and handling complex inquiries from customers are highlighted. So, if the reader is a hiring manager looking to fill a similar role at, say, a coffee shop with a staff of 14 employees, then this employee might be a match. Even though the company types are different – retail (pet care store) instead of food service (coffee shop), most of the highlighted skills would be applicable in either environment. Reading this resume, I would assume this individual enjoys managing a small team of employees and would like to continue doing so in their next job.

Now, let's look at the same job, but this time different responsibilities have been highlighted.

Example 3:

Shift Manager

Primary instructor for new employees about different breeds of pets serviced, including small reptiles, birds, and mammals such as rodents and domestic cats. Managed 4 special pet adoption events per year in terms of staffing and basic animal care inquiries. Additional responsibilities include:

- Recommended products such as food or recreational items based on animal size and breed.
- Administration of staff timesheets, vacation schedules, and coverage for employee illness.
- Completed multiple training hours for basic veterinary assistance.

If you were reading this resume, what would you think this individual is primarily proud of accomplishing? When written this way, it doesn't sound like their interests are with shift management, but rather working directly with animals. Even though everything mentioned in both examples might have been done by the same person, what they've chosen to talk about impacts the way the reader perceives this person's skills. So, if the reader is a hiring manager looking to fill a similar role at, say, a coffee shop with a staff of 14 employees, in this example this resume seems like less of a match. However, if a veterinarian was looking for an office assistant or other entry level role, this person sounds like potentially a good hire!

When it comes to listing accomplishments about your job (which I refer to as "writing bullets"), I recommend the following best practices.

- Numbers are eye-catching. I like to include a number in at least the first bullet for your most recent job. There doesn't need to be a number in every single bullet but try to include at least one.

- Bullets are easier to read than paragraphs. If you're writing more than three sentences talking about a job, then switch to bullets after the first couple of sentences. The goal is to make it easy to read and understand the things that you know how to do and are proud of.

- Awards and recognition can be included as bullets, such as "Employee of the month" or "Top 10 fundraiser" and so on.

- Like the Summary section, bullets should make sense but do not need to be complete sentences. Having said that, I like to end each bullet with a period. It closes out the thought and I believe looks 'polished,' however this is not a grammatical requirement for a resume.

- Don't create a bullet unless you can talk about why you included it.

- Starting bullets with verbs, such as: Organized, Sold, Oversaw, Created, Managed, Stocked, Built, Designed, Serviced, Administered, and so on – tends to make the thought more interesting to read. When using verbs, make sure the verb tense matches from bullet to bullet.

- Use the bullets to showcase your interests. It's not likely that you'll be able to describe every task you did in a job, so instead share what you liked best or were best at and would like to do in the future.

- If you need ideas for what to incorporate into bullets, then think about items from your current job description, or most recent employee review, or any commendations you may have received.

What if you've had a similar job at more than one company? Do you need to repeat the same bullets for each job? No. Once you've mentioned a skill or responsibility there is no need to repeat it unless for some reason you feel this helps your chances of landing a job. So, for example, let's pretend you are applying for a role that asks for at least 5 years of coding experience. You've worked at your current job for 2 years, and then were at your previous company for 4 years and altogether have over 6 years of required experience. In that case I recommend mentioning your coding responsibilities at each job and perhaps even talk about it in your Summary too ("Software development with over 6 years coding experience") in order to make it clear that your skills match the requirement.

Do you need to include bullets and detailed descriptions for every job you've had? This is a great question, and my guidance depends on how much experience you have. So, before I answer this in more detail, let's talk about resume length.

Unless you are in a highly specialized field (and you would know if you are), a resume should be one side of one page if you have less than approximately 5 years' work experience; a page-and-a-half for about 5 to 10 years' work experience, and up to a full two pages (or the front and back of one page) for 10+ years' of experience. Do not try to cram 15 years of incredible experience onto one side of one page, and if you are looking to start your first job ever then do not make the reader scroll or flip to page 2.

With this in mind, adjust how you describe jobs and write bullets accordingly. If you've worked at four companies over the past 12 years then the oldest job listed might only have the company name and brief description, job title and very short explanation of possibly only a single line, and the relevant years. By that point in your resume the reader should have gotten to know you well enough that a job from over a decade ago doesn't make much of an impact on the present day. If there is something from your past that you particularly want to highlight, then of course that is your choice; my guidance is to use the space as it makes sense to describe yourself to the reader.

Should you include volunteer efforts in your work experience section? This is another great question. My advice is to consider whether including this will help you land the job that you want. Sometimes our most valuable experience comes from volunteering; or if we're making a career change then some skills might have been developed in volunteer roles as opposed to previous paying jobs. If you are including volunteer work, then you can format this in the same way in which you would a paying job. Include the name of the organization, your role – which might simply be "Volunteer" – and the dates. If this was a one-time event you can note the year in which it occurred. In the description, talk a little bit about what you did and do include relevant bullets. For a single event you can clarify that this was a "Spring 2023 fundraiser" or "Annual Fall Bowl-a-thon," etc. If your job title does not state that you were a volunteer, then be sure to mention this in the description so that it is clear to the reader.

We've covered a lot of ground in this section, so before we move on to Education, here are some suggestions of what "Not to do" under Work Experience:

A. NO: Months when writing the dates of employment. Years only.

B. NO: Long paragraphs: use bullets to bring attention to important responsibilities, skills, and accomplishments.

C. NO: Salary. You do not need to put this information in writing on your resume.

D. NO: Including inaccurate information. Never misrepresent your skills, responsibilities, or accomplishments. Your resume is about highlighting how wonderful you already are, so there is no need to make things up.

E. NO: Inconsistent formatting. This can look distracting right away and work against you. I recommend creating your resume, then if you have time walking away from it for a few hours or even overnight before giving it a final proof-read. Pay attention to how you have used bold font, capital letters, where the dates are placed, punctuation at the end of bullets, and so on. We all make mistakes, and your resume is your showcase; take the time to do this important review.

F. NO: Too long or too short resumes. Unless you are in a specialized field, resumes are a page to two pages.

G. NO: Bullets just for the sake of writing bullets. Be prepared to talk about every item on your resume and why it is important to you. This is your experience; if a hiring manager asks you about something then you owe it to yourself to provide a thoughtful reply.

Education

Education

The final section of your resume is your Education. The only exception to this is if you are currently a student or have graduated within the last 12 months – in those circumstances then it is okay to put this immediately after your Summary and before Work Experience. This section is short and communicates information about your level of schooling and any degrees.

Example 1:

Education

ACME University   **2003**
Bachelor of Arts, Psychology

Example 2:

EDUCATION

Riverdell Community College   **2024 (anticipated)**
Associates Degree

Example 3:

EDUCATION

South Campus Graduate School   **2008**
Master of Computer Science
Focus on Artificial Intelligence Design

Acme University   **2003**
Bachelor of Science: Computer Science

Formatting the Education section of your resume should follow a similar style to what was used for both the Summary and Work Experience. So, if the previous section titles were centered then make sure that Education is centered as well. If you used bold font for the names of the previous companies that you worked for then use bold again for the name of the school. The title of your degree can follow the same format as job titles.

In the Education section only the graduation year is needed; not the year when you started school. In Example 2 above it shows that the graduation year is anticipated to be in 2024; this informs the reader that this person is currently a student working on their degree, and that they believe this will be completed in 2024. Make sure that when you use the (anticipated) wording that the date is always in the future; this isn't used to indicate that you thought you were going to graduate at some point in the past and then did not.

What if you attended multiple colleges, for example if you began at one school then transferred to another? In that case you only need to include the school from which you graduated; unless you feel there is a strong benefit to including the original school then this information does not need to be on your resume.

What about non-college degrees? If you wish to show a certification or other credential which is not a college diploma, then these can be listed here as well. Follow a similar format as with the schools for consistency. The most recent credential is always listed first. For high school, unless you are a very recent high school graduate then your school's name and the graduation year do not need to be provided.

I generally recommend against listing information such as grade point average, extra-curricular activities, or anything other than your major unless you graduated within the last couple of years. If you are a recent grad who is building your professional work experience then seeing this information can help the reader understand more about you, and what you can contribute to a job. Once you have been working for about 5 years, though, your accomplishments on the job are more recent and therefore more relevant than school.

Here are a couple guidelines for what "Not to do" in the Education section:

A. NO: Overabundance of details. This is the last section of your resume; the reader has learned a lot about you by this point. In this section they are learning a couple final details about your background; there isn't a need to list out every class, hobby, club, and so on. Use that space for your professional experience instead.

B. NO: Inaccurate information. When I worked in Executive Search there would occasionally be a resume claiming that someone had a degree when they did not. Assume that a hiring manager will verify this information, and that you could lose a job if this is not truthful.

And that is how to put together a resume! Congratulations, we've now reviewed each of the sections in detail, and seen multiple examples and talked about best practices. Before we wrap things up by looking at one final template, I'd like to take a moment and talk about what makes a good employee.

I think there is a misconception that unless you were the best in everything, or have won multiple awards, or were consistently the top <<whatever>>, or were in a senior level role, or went to a certain school, or have a certain degree, that you are not as deserving of a job as someone else. I promise, that is not the case.

A "good employee" is someone who is doing what they want to do, at a job that values their skills. The reason I am passionate about helping to write resumes is because everyone looking for a job is worthy of a great resume; meaning a resume which is easy to understand, consistently formatted, and which shows off their experience and potential. There is no reason that only some people should have this information while others do not; so, I hope this book can help level the playing field of well-crafted resumes. YOU can have a resume which stands out from the crowd simply by knowing how to correctly put one together.

So, let's take another look at putting all these pieces together in the following resume example.

Quinn Person's
Resume Example

Resume Example

Header

Quinn Person
<hr>
123 Street Town, State 12345

555 – 555 – 5555   quinnperson14@email.com

Remember to keep the Header to two or three lines. Use accurate contact information which you check regularly so that you can respond in a timely manner. Your email address should be easily recognizable as belonging to you. Unlike every other section of the resume, you do not need to write "Header" above the Header. Start at the top of the page with your name.

Summary

Creative, goal-driven marketing professional with a background in both business and art. Seeking to apply my skills to a small to midsize brand expanding name recognition through innovative use of media.

Briefly describe your talents, experience, and what kind of job you are seeking. When applying to a specific job posting it is helpful to match terms from the job description to your Summary. Sentence fragments are acceptable if the wording makes sense.

Work Experience

Art Collective Company City, State   2019 – Present
Marketing Director: Social Media
Responsible for creating and overseeing successful execution of $1MM annual social media budget. Goal of expanding reach by 150% to target audience. Additional responsibilities and accomplishments include:

- Award for 2021 Most Innovative Ad for "Art Collective is Life" campaign.
- Expanded reach within 5 new countries by 25%.
- Managed team of 5 Marketing Specialists.

Jane Organization City, State   2017 – 2019
Senior Marketing Specialist
Created over 50 pieces of content in both written and online format. Xxxxxxxxxxxxxxxxxxxxxxxx xxxxxxxxxxx

Discuss the WHERE, WHEN, and WHAT of your work experience. Most recent / current job is listed first. Think of each job as answering the "May I Help You?" question by illustrating your skills and accomplishments. Tailor the items you focus on to match the keywords in your Summary; if you're looking for a job in accounting focus on experience working with a billing department or budgeting – even if this is a career change for you. Remember that numbers are eye-catching and starting off bullets with a verb can make what follows more interesting to read. Be ready to talk about anything included in this section; don't add items just for 'filler.' Total resume length should be one page to two pages, commensurate with years of experience.

Education

Liberal Arts University   **2010**
Bachelor of Arts, Fine Arts
Minor in Business Management

Follow similar formatting to your Work Experience section. Include the year of graduation or certificate completion only; start dates are not needed. If you have graduated within the past 12 months or are a current student then this section can precede Work Experience, otherwise it should come last.

Afterword
& Acknowledgements

One Final Thought

Good luck to you! Best wishes in your current and future job searches, and throughout your career. I hope you encounter nothing but success.

And one final recommendation: revisit your resume once a year, in order to keep it up to date. That saves you from potentially having to spend a lot of time making changes all at once. Add in new accomplishments and feel free to adjust your Summary to fit your growth. If you achieve new educational milestones make sure to update those as well.

I hope these resume guidelines have been helpful. Think of me cheering you on! Best of luck!

- Amy

Acknowledgements

I am deeply grateful to anyone who has allowed me to provide feedback on their resume over the past 15+ years. This includes friends, family, friends-of-friends, complete strangers, co-workers, and probably some folks I am forgetting to mention. I do not take your trust in me lightly and am grateful for the opportunity to work with you.

Thank you to my mentors over the years who have made me better. Growth can be uncomfortable, so extra special thanks to those who have challenged me.

Finally, thank you to my wonderful family. You are the most interesting people; I love being able to share my life with you.

www.ingramcontent.com/pod-product-compliance
Lightning Source LLC
Chambersburg PA
CBHW062303290526
45794CB00006B/2682